AWAKE • DESPIERTO

INSIDE ✿ ADENTRO

Opuestos

Mexican Folk Art Opposites in English and Spanish

Cynthia Weill

Wood Sculptures from **Oaxaca** by
Quirino and Martín Santiago

SCHOLASTIC INC.
New York Toronto London Auckland Sydney New Delhi Hong Kong

ASLEEP ✦ DORMIDO

OUTSIDE ✿ AFUERA

HIGH ✿ ALTO

LOW ✿ BAJO

DAY ❁ DÍA

NIGHT ✦ NOCHE

FACE ✦ CARA

TAIL ✿ COLA

LEFT ✱ **IZQUIERDA**

RIGHT ✳ DERECHA

OPEN ✦ ABIERTOS

CLOSED ✿ CERRADOS

BIG ✳ GRANDE

LITTLE ✻ PEQUEÑO

LONG ✤ LARGA

SHORT ✤ CORTA

ALIKE ✤ **I**GUALES

DIFFERENT ✽ DIFERENTES

MANY ✦ MUCHOS

FEW ❖ **POCOS**

FAST ❋ RÁPIDO

SLOW ✳ LENTA

TOGETHER ✤ JUNTOS

APART • SEPARADOS

SITTING ❋ SENTADO

STANDING ✿ PARADO

HELLO ❃ HOLA

GOODBYE ✱ **ADIÓS**

Photo by Joyce M. Grossbard

Bottom row: Cynthia Weill; artisan-in-training, Adal Santiago; Julio Jiménez; Martín Santiago; Quirino Santiago
Top row: Calixto Santiago, Maximinio Santiago, Jaime Santiago, Eloy Santiago, Plácido Santiago.

❀ ❀

Dedication

To Victoria Weill, my dearest friend and advocate.

Thanks to

Casa Colonial, Oaxaca, Mexico, Jane and Thorny Robison, Amado Bolaños, Victor Sánchez, Hector González, Nicholas Boucher, Ann Levine, Jan Asikainen, Myriam Chapman, Graeme Sullivan, Xochítl Medina, Remualdo Bautista, Hank Baker, Janet Glass, Alejandro Ramírez, Irma Ortiz, José Miguel Moracho, Leslie Martino, Ruth Borgman, Arden Rothstein, Mari Haas, Blanca Llaurado, Becky Harmon, Abigail Kanter, K.B. Basseches, Carlomagno Pedro Martínez, Frances Weill, Joyce Grossbard, and the Bank Street Writers Lab.

Very Special Thanks

Nancy Faxon Mygatt

❀ ❀ ❀ ❀ ❀ ❀ ## Photography, Cover, and Book Design ❀ ❀ ❀ ❀ ❀ ❀

Sergio A. Gómez

Copyright © 2009 by Cynthia Weill.
All rights reserved. Published by Scholastic Inc., 557 Broadway, New York, NY 10012, by arrangement with Cinco Puntos Press. Printed in the U.S.A.
ISBN-13: 978-0-545-19861-5   ISBN-10: 0-545-19861-5
SCHOLASTIC and associated logos and designs are trademarks and/or registered trademarks of Scholastic Inc.

17 18 19 20 21 22   40   18 17 16